LOVE MINUS

By
Mary Gallagher

★

★

DRAMATISTS
PLAY SERVICE
INC.

To LYDIA — both of her.

ABOUT THE AUTHOR

Mary Gallagher is a writer/director/actress who has published stories and two novels, SPEND IT FOOLISHLY and QUICK-SILVER.

Her plays FATHER DREAMS, LITTLE BIRD, CHOCO-LATE CAKE, BUDDIES, BEDTIME, DOG EAT DOG, LOVE MINUS and HOW TO SAY GOODBYE have been published by Dramatists Play Service and produced at such theatres as ACT in San Francisco, the Loretto Hilton in St. Louis, Berkshire Theatre Festival, Actors Theatre of Louisville, Hartford Stage, Theatre Three in Dallas, the Victory Gardens and the Next Theatre in Chicago, the Main Street Theater and the Alley Theatre in Houston, and the Sanctuary Theatre in Washington; in New York at the Ark Theatre Company, the Ensemble Studio Theatre, the Vineyard Theatre, Home for Contemporary Theatre and Art and the American Place Theatre; at the Abbey Theatre in Dublin; and in Australia and Canada.

CHOCOLATE CAKE won the Heidemann Award at the 1981 Humana Festival and was produced Off-Broadway in 1983 at the Provincetown Playhouse as part of an evening called WIN/LOSE/DRAW, co-authored by Ara Watson.

Gallagher and Watson also wrote the CBS-TV movie NOBODY'S CHILD, starring Marlo Thomas and directed by Lee Grant, for which they won a Christopher Award, a Luminas Award from Women In Film, and the Writers Guild Award for Outstanding Achievement in 1986.

Ms. Gallagher's other film and television credits include LOVE/RUN, a feature for MGM; A DIFFERENT ROMANCE, a TV movie for CBS and Josephy Feury; an episode of the ABC series HOTHOUSE; and a comedy development deal with Embassy TV.

Ms Gallagher has received grants from the Office For Advanced Drama Research and the National Endowment for the Humanities; a New Dramatists residency at the Tyrone Guthrie Centre in Ireland; and playwriting fellowships from the Guggenheim Foundation (1983), the Rockefeller Foundation (1984), the National Endowment for the Arts (1987), and the New York Foundation for the Arts (1988). She was co-winner of the 1986 Susan Smith Blackburn Prize for HOW TO SAY GOODBYE.

Recent projects include a series of short pieces for THE HOME SHOW: V and VI, and ¿DE DÓNDE?, a new play about Central American refugees in the Rio Grande Valley of Texas, which was recently workshopped at the Alley Theatre in Houston and at River Arts in Woodstock. In October, Ms. Gallagher directed the premiere at the Main Street Theater in Houston.

Ms. Gallagher is an alumna of New Dramatists and a member of the Ensemble Studio Theatre and the Dramatists Guild.

LOVE MINUS was read many times as it was developed, and workshopped by Capitol Rep at Art Awareness in Lexington, New York in 1988. The playwright would like to thank New Dramatists, the Hudson Guild Theatre and the Ensemble Studio Theatre, where the play was read, and the many actors who read it, especially Christine Lavren, Stephanie Cassel and Geoffrey Wade.

THE SET

A unit set, clean and very simple, accommodating side-by-side scenes in Karla's and Nick's apartments and separate scenes at center in Lydia's office. This should be accomplished with an abstract design, a few places to sit—also something like a studio couch in Karla's apartment—and a large window frame at Center, which can be hung with different curtains, plants, stained glass, etc., to establish change of scene. The props are stored inside the units or brought on and off by actors. The action is continuous, with voices bridging scenes.

THE CHARACTERS

The characters are all approaching 30.

KARLA
LYDIA
NICK
ALAN

The action takes place over a period of about three months, in New York City.

THE SCENES

LOVE MINUS

ACT ONE
Scene I

A promenade along the Hudson River.

Karla is leaning on a railing, looking at the water, daydreaming. Nick enters, strolling, approaches her, leans on the railing. Friendly, offhand:

NICK. Hi. *(Karla slowly focuses, looks at him.)*
KARLA. *(Uncertain.)* Were you...?
NICK. Yeah.
KARLA. Hi ... Do I know you?
NICK. *(Surprised.)* No.
KARLA. Oh, good, okay.
NICK. Sorry. *(Starts to go.)*
KARLA. Oh no, I wasn't ... I just wondered.
NICK. ... Yeah?
KARLA. Yeah, really, no. I just ... I do that sometimes. Fail to know people. People I *know*, it's terrible, so...
NICK. Oh. Right. Yeah ... No, I just said hi.
KARLA. Oh... Hi. *(Pause. They look back at the river. She starts fading off again, but:)*
NICK. It's great out here, isn't it? Almost like ... not New York.
KARLA. I know.

9

NICK. First star.

KARLA. Where? *(Nick points. She gives a little laugh. Amazing.)*

NICK. I know.

KARLA. You just forget about them! And all the time, they're here for us ... the stars, the river...

NICK. Yeah ... But, you know ... we're here. We made it!

KARLA. Finally!

NICK. And they're still here. So...

KARLA. Yeah ... and the whole city falls away...

NICK. This is what matters, right. *(Pause.)*

KARLA. Are you in real estate?

NICK. *(Startled.)* No.

KARLA. Good. No, it just seems like everybody is, these days.

NICK. Oh. Right. You're not an actress, are you?

KARLA. *(Amused.)* Me? God, no!

NICK. I'm an actor.

KARLA. *(Embarrassed.)* Oh. Oh, well, listen, I can't talk, I'm a writer.

NICK. Screenplays?

KARLA. No. Nothing that might actually make real money. Stories.

NICK. Huh. But they get like, published?

KARLA. Well ... some do ... somewhere ... sometime...

NICK. So you get paid?

KARLA. ... You *can* ... I guess I'm not in it for the rewards, I just can't seem to stop.

NICK. Huh.

KARLA. But still ... when I'm in the middle of it, it's my whole reality, it completely eats me up, and I'm ... I'm so *happy!*

NICK. Yeah! Yeah, right! For those moments ... it's all worth it. Anything, you know?

KARLA. You get that in the theatre too?

NICK. Well ... you can, it happens...

KARLA. *(Shy, blurts.)* I just wrote a book. I hope. I finished it tonight. I hope. I mean I did. I mailed it. So I hope it's a book. And

10

I hope it's finished. But it could be just embarrassing.

NICK. You mean like a novel? *(She nods.)* That's great, that's terrific! How long did it take you, years? *(She nods.)* God, and you just finished it? You must feel fantastic!

KARLA. Actually, I feel like I'm coming down with something.

NICK. Yeah, sure! Yeah, I always do that too, when a show is over.

KARLA. Because your work is gone?

NICK. I guess. Getting sick ... it fills the time ... cause suddenly there's all this *time!* And you get so *lonely!*

KARLA. Yes! That thing has been my whole life, really ... for so long! And now it's gone! What in the hell will I *do?*

NICK. I'll tell you. You should celebrate.

KARLA. Yeah ... well ... I don't know...

NICK. No, that's one thing I know! You gotta take the chance to be happy when it's there, because it gets so tough again, so fast...

KARLA. Wow, that's the truth...

NICK. So ... seize the day! You know?

KARLA. You're right, no, I do think you're right. It's just ... I guess I haven't quite let go of it. That's very hard for me. You know, when you invest so much...

NICK. Well, sure! And this is your first novel, right? It's like a breakthrough? It could change your life? *(She nods, laughing, anxious.)* You're jumping off the high dive! God, that's the best, I live for that! I'm buying you champagne!

KARLA. Oh, no, please, you don't have to—

NICK. Are you kidding? Now I'm excited too! I mean, you know ... I never knew a novelist!

KARLA. Well, I'm not that great to know, I'm always in my room.

NICK. Not now.

KARLA. *(Laughs, nervous.)* ... Well, no ... for once!...

NICK. And I'm at loose ends too. This was my last day on a show. And Christ, I mean, I'm like, *released,* I couldn't wait! But still ... you know...

11

KARLA. You're feeling a little bit congested?

NICK. Yeah, maybe kind of feverish—

KARLA. We do need an activity.

NICK. So we're gonna drink champagne ... and talk about our dreams. *(Beat, as she looks at him, beginning to take in the fact that something's happening here.)*

KARLA. That's so nice. Thank you.

NICK. *(Grins.)* Thank *you*. *(Beat; then:)* This is great. When you really look at me. You have amazing eyes.

KARLA. "Amazing?" Why?

NICK. *(Laugh.)* Why? *(Crossfade as music in and their voices are heard:)*

Scene II

We hear Karla's and Nick's voices first.

KARLA. That was your *name?* "*Brent Winstead*"!

NICK. I know, it sounds like I was born in the middle of a polo game.

KARLA. "Brent Winstead"! Oh my God!

NICK. Hey, I had to *be* this guy! They tell you, 'We want you to play Brent Winstead," and your blood runs cold.

(Lights up on Karla's studio apartment. It's three days later, afternoon. They're on the daybed, half-dressed.)

KARLA. Well, now I've got to see this—

NICK. Like hell you will, you don't have a television — I still can't believe that, you're not living in America — anyway, I'm off the soap.

KARLA. You said your death scene is next week — I'll go to a bar and watch it—

NICK. *(Laughs.)* What?! They don't watch soaps in bars—
KARLA. Come on, this is New York! I bet there are special bars where people go to watch the soaps — on those huge TV screens—
NICK. *(Laughing but repulsed.)* Oh, Christ! — Really, please. Don't watch it, okay?
KARLA. *(Surprised.)* Okay ... if ... Why?
NICK. ... Look ... I'm not ashamed of what *I* do, I can make it work, okay? Anything they give me, but .... it's what they make me say.
KARLA. Like what?
NICK. "Tell me, Hilary ... does that old cellar door still lead to the basement?"
KARLA. Oh, you're kidding—
NICK. And millions of people hear me say this asinine—
KARLA. Oh, do another one!
NICK. Okay ... this was like, last week ... "You should have seen her, Nicola. She looked like she'd been through hell. Her eyes, were so ... tormented! Her clothes were torn ... her hair was wild ... she didn't even have a purse."
KARLA. ... "She didn't even have a *purse*"...?
NICK. Yeah, I guess that's the worst thing that can happen to you, it's like a sign of total breakdown—
KARLA. Wow, that's great, you should keep a record of that stuff—
NICK. Well, most of it's not even funny, it's just ... really phony. I'm spose to be in love, in this *asshole* way, my character—
KARLA. "Brent"? *(He looks at her.)* I'm sorry ... really, tell me...
NICK. No, nothing, it's just ... so I'm in love, so I have to go on and on about it. And I sound exactly like these greeting cards I get from these pathetic fans ... you know, the couple, like, in silhouettes, with the sunset ... and inside it says ... "You are the parasol in the Mai-Tai of my life," or some ... That's the way I talk! Even when I'm dying, I'm gasping out that garbage! It's just ... it's humiliating! And I kept telling the writers, "When you really feel something,

you don't talk about it!" Right?

KARLA. ... I don't know. Sometimes I'm so amazed at what I feel, I just *have* to say it! *(Beat; then, shyly.)* I'm amazed right now. *(Nick looks at her, then smiles, then gets up, starts to dress.)*

NICK. *You're* pretty amazing, how you just come out with things.

KARLA. Well, I'm alone too much, my manners are all shot to hell. But listen... if you hate it that much... why are you on this soap opera?

NICK. *(Disbelief.)* You've heard of money?

KARLA. Oh. Well, sure—

NICK. But not *just* that, I mean ... *(Trails off, too complicated.)* When you're an actor, most of what you do is crap. You wanta work, you learn to hold your nose. *(She doesn't understand.)* See, actors ... all we ever talk about is, "Hey, I'm working, are you working?" Like that's everything! And it *is!* Someone like my roommate Alan, God, I mean he *never* works, except... like, this kid show tour he's out with ... and now I work a lot, you know? Al thinks I've got it knocked! But in a way, it's harder now, because ... you can't let down, you gotta keep that motor going, crank it up and get out there and make it happen, man! It's like, no matter what you're doing, part of your mind is wondering what you're missing out on. When you're on the coast, you wonder if it'd be better here, and when you're here, you're thinking, shit, why aren't I on the coast? It's like you're juggling all the time, and you feel like if you drop one ball, the whole thing might go... *(Gestures: KABLOOEY!)* And at night, you know, you can't just shut it down ... I get really nuts sometimes, trying to unwind...

KARLA. ... I guess.

NICK. So I'll say, to hell with it, today I'm gonna blow it off, forget the business, just...! So I go to the park, or down to the river, maybe, like the night we met ... and, you know, it's beautiful, I'm starting to let go ... and then I see another actor. And my guts start churning. And I don't want to do it, but I'm doing it. "What's happening? What are you up for? Hey, I'm working! Are you working?" Christ! *(Beat; then, continues.)* You don't relate to this at all,

14

you think it's slimey.

KARLA. ... No ... but I—

NICK. I'll tell you something else — I've been an actor since I was in high school, and my father has never seen me in a play. He just didn't think it mattered. But the first day I was on the soap, he stayed home from work to watch it.

KARLA. God.

NICK. So now you think my father is an asshole, right? *(Slight pause.)* Sorry ... God. I'm sorry ... I...

KARLA. *(Uncertain for the first time.)* What's the matter, Nick?

NICK. I don't know ... I'm tired, you know? I mean, I am shot! I've been here since ... Thursday? Jesus, you'd think we were seventeen.

KARLA. Seventeen was a nightmare! This is nice!

NICK. *(Grins.)* "Nice?" Good.

KARLA. *(Reassured.)* "Nice!" It's unbelievable!

NICK. *(Bothered.)* Oh, yeah?

KARLA. Not now. But I didn't trust you at first, you know. Well, you *are* an actor. *(Sees that this hits him hard.)* Just at first! You were so sure, so fast! And I—

NICK. I never said a word to you that wasn't—

KARLA. Nick, you must know I trust you now ... after this last time we made love ... *(Slight pause. Nick's really bothered now, but trying not to be, goes back to gathering his stuff.)*

NICK. I gotta admit, it kinda threw me ... when you cried like that...

KARLA. It scared me too ... to feel so much ... I guess I had a lot saved up. I hope it didn't...

NICK. What?

KARLA. ... Make you ... uneasy, or...

NICK. *(Uneasy.)* No, I mean ... hey, it happened, so...

KARLA. Well, I won't do that to you again—

NICK. Look, don't worry, it's no big deal, okay? *(Sits next to her, takes her hand.)* You're fading too. I gotta get some sleep — and eat, you hardly ever eat!

KARLA. Well, not formally — I'm sorry — Oh, wait! *(Gets thick*

15

manila envelope, gives it to him, saying.) You wanted to read it, so...

NICK. Wow ... thanks. I'll be real careful with it.

KARLA. I don't care, eat lunch on it, but you better like it!

NICK. *(Laughs.)* Right... now look, I might not call you right away — things are pretty crazy, I'm up for a film that's like, shooting in Pymatuning, Pennsylvania, or some crazy place — and there's something on the coast — but as soon as I know where I'm at—

KARLA. I'm not worried. *(He stops, looks at her a beat, kisses her briefly and sweetly. Music in, crossfade to:)*

Scene III

LYDIA'S OFFICE.

In the dark, we hear the voices of Karla and Lydia.

KARLA. I nearly passed out when I saw the prices! I couldn't do it, I *refused!*

LYDIA. What?! Oh no—

KARLA. — I walked out, twice—

LYDIA. — I knew I should've dragged you by the hand—

KARLA. — but then I thought, "Oh God, I'll be wearing that jacket I bought in college till the day I die!" So I went back!

LYDIA. Thank God!

(Lights up. Karla has a large Macy's shopping bag, is spilling tissue paper and underpants in exotic colors all over the place.)

KARLA. I bought fourteen pairs!

LYDIA. Good Lord!

KARLA. *(Apologetic.)* Well, you know, I may never do this again—

LYDIA. — No, it's great — ooh, nice! *(Feels fabric.)*

KARLA. And with fourteen pairs, I'll save on laundry—

LYDIA. — Don't ruin it! What else? *(Karla holds up a dress.)* Mm, pretty ... a little "TV wife"...

KARLA. *(Stung.)* I can't just start out in the nightie.

LYDIA. A nightie? Where, let's see.

KARLA. *(Fishing nightie out of bag.)* It's been months — I have to work us up to this—

LYDIA. No, I know, I know ... *(As nightie emerges, holds it up.)* Oh, *fabulous!*

KARLA. *(Smiling, nervous.)* Well, I don't know...

LYDIA. *What,* you don't know?

KARLA. It doesn't feel like me—

LYDIA. Right, it's terrific!

KARLA. ... I guess with the other stuff...

LYDIA. There's more? *(Digs in bag.)*

KARLA. Once I started, I just spiralled — it was like a fit!

LYDIA. *(In bag.)* Perfume ... bath oil ... what a gas ... what's this? New sheets? Good move. The color's kind of ... eh...

KARLA. But feel them.

LYDIA. *(Looks at her, then feels sheets.)* Satin sheets?!

KARLA. I saw the sign, my mind went blank, all I could see was those old Harlow movies with the huge beds, and I heard my voice say, "I want those!"

LYDIA. *(Throwing arms around Karla.)* I'M SO PROUD OF YOU!

KARLA. I SPENT THE RENT!

LYDIA. Hey, this is an investment, you can take this off your income tax! God, I'm excited! Wadaya want to drink?

KARLA. *(Abandon.)* Absinthe!

LYDIA. You got it. *(Shows her absinthe bottle.)*

KARLA. What? No.

LYDIA. Oui. My Fearless Leader, Fred. He got some jerk from France to procure it for him. Except he finally opened it, and he doesn't like it. *(Laughs rudely.)*

KARLA. What's it taste like?

LYDIA. Like the stuff they pour into the Xerox smells. Want some?

KARLA. No. *(Happily.)* I don't know what I want!

LYDIA. Vermouth. Want to order up ethnic? *(Gets out glasses and vermouth.)*

KARLA. Sure. Oh. No. I spent all my—

LYDIA. Don't worry about it—

KARLA. Lydia, I don't want you always paying—

LYDIA. When you're famous, I'll exploit *you.*

KARLA. Yeah, you think you're kidding. But if I ever do get rich, you can do anything you want!

LYDIA. God, how terrifying! *(She pours two huge tumblers of vermouth, emptying the bottle. Karla starts folding clothes in tissue, replacing them in bag.)*

KARLA. ... Oh God, oh God ... I hope this turns out the way I picture it!

LYDIA. It's always worth a shot.

KARLA. Oh, yeah? What if he disappears again?

LYDIA. Well hell, they all do *that.*

KARLA. Well, I sure didn't see it coming. Those three days we were lovers ... okay, it was only three days — but three days *straight!*

LYDIA. *(Impressive.)* Hey. *(Messes with ice and lemon.)*

KARLA. It was all so perfect! The kind of romance you think you'll never get to have!

LYDIA. No shit.

KARLA. And then he disappeared! For *months!* God, I thought I'd die!

LYDIA. But he came back. So go with it — *(Hands Karla her drink.)*

KARLA. *(Huge drink.)* My God!—

LYDIA. Just don't expect too much. *(Drinks.)*

KARLA. Oh, it's all so weird! I'd really started hating him ... thinking he was a phony, and ... *(Hard to admit.)* not even very *bright* ... and then I heard his voice on the phone and, I mean ... I got *cramps.*

LYDIA. Poor baby. Well, you hadn't had a lover in years, no wonder—

KARLA. What?! No! Not ... *years*, good grief, I'm not that—

LYDIA. Yeah?

KARLA. *(Struggling.)* ... Well ... certainly some *time* ... but it wasn't like I missed it! I thought I was through with all that passionate, romantic—

LYDIA. What a crock.

KARLA. I did! I thought I was content! I like to live alone ... I had my friends, I had my work ... and when I'm working ... my work is all I think about ... and I'm practically always working, so...

LYDIA. So there you have it, folks.

KARLA. And anyway, I don't believe that every woman has to have some man in her life to be content. *(Looks at Lydia. No comment.)* I don't! and I *was* content!

LYDIA. You were starting to turn into Emily Dickinson.

KARLA. What a rotten thing to say!

LYDIA. So this guy's not reliable — well, Christ, who is? At least he woke you up!

KARLA. *(Bursts out.)* I wish I could sleep with him right now and get it over with!

LYDIA. ..."Get it over with?"

KARLA. Well, the *build-up* is killing me—

LYDIA. You're the one who made him wait! "Start all over, get to be real friends before you screw again," all that crap—

KARLA. And I was right! We are real friends now!

LYDIA. Jesus Christ, you're courting!

KARLA. God, and he's so patient! We always end up back at my place, you know ... drinking wine ... and for me, that's fatal, I have one drink around Nick and all I want to do is...

LYDIA. Honey, don't tell *me.*

KARLA. But Nick will drink and talk with me till two o'clock in the morning ... and he says the most wonderful things to me, so ... you know ... so *loving* ... but then he just ... goes home.

LYDIA. *(Thinks it's all insane.)* Well?! You made the rules!

KARLA. Yeah, but now I'm ready!

19

LYDIA. Clarify your signals. Show him your underwear.

KARLA. *(Not hearing.)* ... God, Lydia. I might get to have everything — my work, my friends, and love.

LYDIA. Gee, kid, it's a dream come true.

KARLA. Well, you could have all that too—

LYDIA. Hey, I don't *want* some agonized affair that's gonna turn my insides out! I just want the occasional lightweight lay. Like good old Robert.

KARLA. Robert? Which one ... The bleeder?

LYDIA. True, I'm not about to get satin sheets while I'm screwing a guy who gets nosebleeds when he comes.

KARLA. I don't know where you get these guys. You check them out first, don't you? I mean ... they're safe—

LYDIA. Oh yes, the seals have not been tampered with—

KARLA. I am *serious*—

LYDIA. Please don't start a crusade here—

KARLA. But you can do so much better than creeps like—

LYDIA. Robert may not measure up to your romantic standards—

KARLA. Well, he's married, isn't he? *Apart* from—

LYDIA. He thinks I'm terrific! He says I'm the only woman with brains that he still likes to fuck! Now that's something, isn't it? I'm allowed to have that!

KARLA. But ... don't you want much more than that?

LYDIA. Well, try and get it!

KARLA. I am trying! Does that bother you? *(Pause. Both regret this.)*

LYDIA. Shit ... Let's order, okay? And then we'll plan your strategy.

KARLA. I don't want to plan it. *(Self-mocking.)* I want it to happen. Beautifully!

LYDIA. *(Laughs.)* Oh, Christ!

KARLA. He's coming over tomorrow night! *(Clutches Lydia's arm: Help!)*

LYDIA. No candles, nothing blatant. *Lots* of wine.

KARLA. Champagne!

LYDIA. My my ... and then ... the bath oil, the perfume, the dress
... the karma of the underwear ... he'll have to make the move!
KARLA. *But!*
LYDIA. *But!* If he doesn't, *ask* him! "Hey! You want to do it
or what?"
KARLA. That's finesse.
LYDIA. That's class. *(Crossfade to:)*

Scene IV

KARLA'S APARTMENT.

*The next night. At the window are faded curtains, handmade
from a sheet. Nick sits on the studio couch, pouring two glasses
of champagne. He has a leatherbound volume of poetry.*

NICK. This is great, we both bought champagne. We can drink
one ... reassess the situation ... drink the other one...
KARLA'S VOICE. *(Offstage.)* Oh, God...
NICK. *(Picks up book, leafs through.)* Okay ... now all this stuff is
new to me, so should I just pick one?
KARLA'S VOICE. *(Offstage.)* Sure. Oh, Nick, these are so
beautiful! ... the colors are...
NICK. I thought they looked like you. *(Karla enters, self-conscious
in her new dress and makeup. She carries simple, pretty flowers in a
jar.)*
KARLA. Had to fake the vase. *(Moves her hands to show the peanut
butter label on the jar.)*
NICK. *(Laughs, then.)* Nice dress. *(She sets down the jar, picks up her
glass, sits nearish to Nick on the studio couch as, "casually":)*
KARLA. Thanks. It's part of my new image.
NICK. I always liked your old one.
KARLA. Read. *(Nick gets comfortable, reads a poem at random.)*

21

NICK.
"The heart asks pleasure first,
And then, excuse from pain.
And then, those little anodynes
That deaden suffering.

And then, to go to sleep.
And then, if it should be
The will of its inquisitor,
The liberty to die."
(A reflective pause, then:) That's depressing.
KARLA. ... Well ... but ... it's true, isn't it? ... I mean ... given ...
certain .... and her *style*, of course is ... *(As Nick nods solemnly.)*
Her poems aren't ususally that bleak.
NICK. Yeah, here's a cheery one. *(Reads.)*
"I felt a funeral in my brain,
And mourners, to and fro,
Kept treading, treading, till it seemed
That sense was breaking through—"
KARLA. Give me that! *(Grabs book, leafs through it.)* ... Okay ...
well, no...
NICK. See?
KARLA. Just wait a minute ... all right. *(Nick leans back beside her,
watching her.)*
"Hope is the thing with feathers
That perches in the soul,
And sings the tune without the words,
And never stops at all.

And sweetest in the gale is heard,
And sore must be the storm
That could abash the little bird
That kept so many warm..."
(She trails off, self-conscious, looks at him.)
NICK. Yeah, but look at the one right next to it. *(Reads.)*
"Before I got my eye put out—"

KARLA. *(Jumps up.)* Stop! Stop! You're going to ruin her! ... I never should have told you she's my favorite.

NICK. Why? ... Just because her poems are sad?

KARLA. Her poems ... yeah...

NICK. And what? ... Her life, too?

KARLA. Listen. Here. *(Gives him book.)* It's a beautiful edition, you don't deserve it.

NICK. It's for you.

KARLA. What? No—

NICK. Of course, come on. You'd read 'em, wouldn't you? Just for the hell of it. "Think I'll read a poem."

KARLA. Well ... yeah...

NICK. Yeah, see, I wouldn't. I'd want to , maybe, but ... *(Moves close to show inscription.)* Anyway, it's got your name in it. And ... *(She reads silently: "Love, Nick." A still moment, then:)*

KARLA. *(softly.)* I'd love to have them.

NICK. Good. *(Moves away.)* Hey, it'll be nice for me to think of you, in the evenings, reading poetry ... sipping sherry, maybe...

KARLA. *(Laughs.)* Sherry? Please. Why not Ovaltine?

NICK. Well, you're the only one I know who'd kill time reading poetry.

KARLA. It's not that old world, really—

NICK. It *is* old world, believe me. Look at this place — no media! It's like it's 1890! *(Flops back, relaxing.)* That's why it's so peaceful. All my craziness just stops when I walk in that door. I feel ... I don't know, strange feeling. Like I don't care if I ever work again.

KARLA. ... That's nice.

NICK. You know, that night on the promenade ... I watched you for the longest time before I spoke to you.

KARLA. ... Oh, yeah?

NICK. Yeah. Here were all these people in the park ... little kids on bicycles and ... *radios,* joggers, people with *dogs* ... and in the middle of them, there you were, so *still* ... leaning on the rail, just looking at the water ... like you didn't need the world at all. *(Brief pause. Holding her gaze.)* And when you said you were a writer, I thought ... yeah, she's got her *own* world, she dreams it every day!

23

Really living in a world that you create yourself ... that's what I wanted in the theatre! But it's not like that! Anything that starts like that ... as perfect as a dream ... it never lasts, not in *my* life! And I wanted to ask you that night ... what's the secret? How do you make it last, the dream?

KARLA. *(As he holds her gaze.)* ... I don't know.

NICK. You know. *(Slight pause. He doesn't make the move, so:)*

KARLA. I bought myself a present.

NICK. ... Yeah? *(She moves the couch cover, touches. his hand to the sheet underneath. Thrown:)* ... What ... what is it...?

KARLA. Satin.

NICK. What? The *sheet?*

KARLA. Mm-hm.

NICK. *(Smiles, uncertain.)* ... God ... that must feel incredible ... all over, I mean...

KARLA. Yes, it does. *(Pause. Nothing happens. Karla makes the slightest move toward kissing him. He stops her by:)*

NICK. Karla ... you don't...?

KARLA. What?

NICK. *(Very awkward.)* You don't still ... want us to be lovers?

KARLA. *(Stunned; beat, then:)* ... Yes, I do...

NICK. ... I ... thought ... I don't feel that. *(Beat, then she rises quickly. Nick grabs her wrist, saying:)* Wait, wait — ... *(She jerks her hand away but doesn't move away. Beat; then:)* I didn't mean for this to happen.

KARLA. I don't understand.

NICK. I guess I wasn't ... didn't—

KARLA. Why did you come back, if you didn't want—?

NICK. I *did!* I mean, I thought... but I, it's different now, isn't it? Don't you feel different? *(She looks at him, bewildered.)* I mean we didn't even know each other when we fell in love. But now ... I feel like I really love you — you, the person, Karla! God, that's so much better, isn't it? And that will last, it won't get wrecked, like—

KARLA. But that's what we want, isn't it? ... to be friends and lovers too?

NICK. Yeah ... but ... you're practically my best friend now, you

24

know more about me than ... but I don't know, the closer we get, the more I lose all that romantic stuff...

KARLA. *(With dread.)* Is it something about me that—?

NICK. No! Christ, there's nothing wrong with you! It's just... this sounds idiotic ... but you're completely different from this ... I don't know, I guess "perfect woman" that I have this image of ... and maybe that's all crap, you know, and it'll never happen! But the night we met — it was like a dream, that meeting! And I felt, yeah, this is it, finally, this is the one! I mean, I was so happy ... but... that feeling ... didn't last. *(Brief pause.)* I handled this all wrong. But we *are* friends now, aren't we? Can't we just get past this and—

KARLA. Nick. *(He stops, waits. Very controlled:)* See ... that isn't what I thought was happening.

NICK. No, I know that now.

KARLA. *(Beat; then has to say it.)* I think you knew before.

NICK. ... Well, I ... wasn't sure...

KARLA. *(Abruptly.)* I can't talk about this—

NICK. *(Rising.)* No, sure, I'll go, and you can call me when—

KARLA. And take that book.

NICK. Karla ... Jesus, are you gonna hate me now?

KARLA. ... I have to think. *(Shaken, Nick takes the book, exits. Long beat: she doesn't move. Crossfade to:)*

Scene V

MAN'S VOICE. *(Bureaucrat.)* You next? Got the receipt? Can't give you cash, you get a credit slip. I know, I'm broke, too, lady. Reason for returning? ... No use for it? Okay, and what's the item? ... *Satin sheets?* Wow, that must feel incredible—

KARLA'S VOICE. *(Coldly.)* Just write the goddamn thing.

(Lights up on Karla's apartment, the middle of the day. Karla is in an old, battered-looking bathrobe, the pockets full of kleenex, is blowing her

nose, sullenly. Lydia wears a coat, has just come in.)

LYDIA. Well, what the hell is wrong with him?
KARLA. Or with me—
LYDIA. — Now don't you do that!
KARLA. Now that he really knows me, I don't turn him on?!
LYDIA. But that doesn't mean it's *you*—
KARLA. He walked out the door and my sinuses exploded. And I burned my arm this morning, making *toast* ... I feel so adolescent! I just want to lie in bed and play old mushy records.
LYDIA. Don't have a psychotic break, here, he's not worth that—
KARLA. You don't know! I can't even blame him, really, he can't help the way he feels—
LYDIA. Yeah, but ... don't you think he knew you—
KARLA. Yeah, I, that's the weirdest part, I do feel like he sort of set me up. But maybe that's just me, because what would he get out of that?
LYDIA. If he didn't want to screw, what's he been doing camping on your goddamn doorstep all this time?
KARLA. He wants us to be friends.
LYDIA. Well, fuck that. You *have* friends. *(Karla starts to cry. Lydia puts an arm around her.)* Ohhh...
KARLA. I just wish I knew what he's really feeling...

(Lights up on Nick in his apartment. He's deep in thought. Trying this out:)

NICK. You ... you are the most ... my favorite person, Karla ... *(Listens to that. Tries again:)* You're the only woman that I've felt this way about ... *(What a cliché! Tries again:)* Being with you ... makes me feel like a better person ... *(True, but lame. One more try:)* I miss you all the time ... *(Trails off, very troubled. Lights maintain in both areas as:)*
LYDIA. You've gotta kiss him off.
KARLA. For good? I don't think I can.

26

LYDIA. Just tell him, "You're okay for sex, but I wouldn't have you as a friend." *(Karla chews on this as:)*

NICK. See, you think I don't care for you ... but I do, I care so much ... that's why I can't just ... sex is so ... you're so much more to me than ... shit. *(Sinks into gloom.)*

KARLA. But if I wouldn't have him as a friend ... why would I be in love with him? *(Lydia shrugs: oh, well, that!)* No, I know what I feel. I want everything I got from him those first three days!

LYDIA. But now he likes you too much to get it up. That jerk!

KARLA. Oh, let's not talk about it—

LYDIA. *(Overlapping.)* You are *not* seeing him again!

KARLA. I have to see him one more time, he's got my manuscript.

LYDIA. Doesn't your agent have a copy?

KARLA. Yes. But Nick has *my* copy. I want that back, at least.

LYDIA. Listen, I'll get it from him. I'd like to get a look at that—

KARLA. No, I don't want you trampling on him — ... Oh. *(An idea; looks at Lydia.)* He has a roommate who's been away ... but if he's back ...

(Lights down on them.)

ALAN'S VOICE. *(Offstage.)* Nick? You home?

NICK. In here. *(Alan enters, with duffel bag. He's been away for a rugged month, is shot. Nick tries to rally.)*

ALAN. Hey.

NICK. Hey! My man! Welcome home! How was it?

ALAN. You got my postcards?

NICK. Yeah, the Last Supper with the moving eyeballs was deluxe.

ALAN. Well, that says it all. And man, those kids out in the

27

sticks are strong! They threw things at us — anvils, cows ... anything to eat? *(Exits into kitchen, continues:)* I'm starving, I'll eat anything but grits, I've got grits coating every coil of my intestines, it must look like the Carlsbad Caverns in there ... *(From offstage.)* You famous yet?
NICK. No.
ALAN'S VOICE. *(Offstage.)* Good. Fridge looks great. Sandblasted in here, huh?
NICK. Aren't there eggs or something?
ALAN'S VOICE. *(Offstage.)* Something. Something ... in a bowl? *(Nick winces, recognizing this description. Alan enters with a bowl, a spoon and salt.)*
NICK. You're not gonna eat that?
ALAN. I'll sit with it till I get over my fear, and *then* I'll eat it. *(Alan flops down, limp, sighs.)*
NICK. Another fabulous theatrical experience?
ALAN. The best. The first day, we all loved each other so much, we hugged all day long in the car. And then ... four weeks, nine states, forty-sevens shows. By the end of the tour, we were hugging the doors, I've got bruises from the handles. Plus this new techie — *Rory,* his name is — got to drive. Which woulda been all right, I mean at least he had a license, but he never had to piss. So he wouldn't make the rest stops. And he was such a rude creep that the girls were afraid to tell him when they had to go. So they'd tell this other guy and me and we'd put the muscle on Rory. By the third day out, we didn't even talk to him. We'd see a restroom sign, this other guy would strangle Rory ... and I'd steer us off the road. *(Acts out this whole maneuver.)*
NICK. *(Gloomy, preoccupied.)* Sounds like a whole tour about toilets.
ALAN. Every tour is a tour about toilets! You have to eat and you have to piss, and you cling to that! ... You also have to drink — what else was there to do in a town like Cannery, Missouri? — and we'd get stinking drunk, because we had nothing to say to each other. And the next morning, we'd rise at dawn to do "Foofoo and the Princess of the Sunflower Town." I'd walk into this silo, or

wherever they'd penned up the kids, and I'd say... *(Very weary and hungover.)* "Hi, kids... I'm Mr. Magic Man... can you say Hi?" And they'd all holler, 'HIIIIIII, MIIIIISTER MAAAAAAAAGIC MAAAAAAAN!!!!!'" *(Clutches his head.)* If there's a hell where actors go, it must be children's theatre.

NICK. I don't know how you can do that shit.

ALAN. *(Slightly offended.)* I want to work in the business. *(Nick looks at him.)* Okay, it's embarrassing, the pay is shit, and it's making me hate kids. What do you think I should do instead?

NICK. There are other acting jobs—

ALAN. There are other actors, too, in case you haven't noticed. I ran into a guy I went to NYU with, he was doing a mime on the street. Nobody gave him a goddamn dime. Including me. He's a lousy mime. But he's a damn good actor. He just isn't *cute*. *(Nick knows this is aimed at him, but lets it pass.)* When I told him I was off to tour the rural south with "Foofoo and the Princess of the Sunflower Town," I thought he'd laugh, or puke, or something. But he got this look ... this *look*, you know? ... and he said, "Alan, great. You're *working!*" *(Pause. Both gloomy now.)* We got any peanut butter?

NICK. No. Al—

ALAN. Don't start about lending me money again — it's no solution, Nick! I mean ... you know. Thanks. But if they want me to go out next tour, I'm gonna do it! ... Except they've gotta get somebody else to do the laundry. *(Slight pause.)*

NICK. Al...

ALAN. What.

NICK. ... Does it seem like ... when you tell someone ... a woman ... what you ... how you feel about her ... you know, *love* words ... even when you really mean it ... don't you think it always sounds like crap? *(Pause. Alan is thrown. Finally:)*

ALAN. I don't know, I haven't said it all that much. *(Nick starts to rise and leave.)* No, hey, that's ... that wasn't ... *(Nick stops, looks at him.)* It's just ... you know ... What's goin' on?

NICK. *(Very confused, struggling:)* I don't know. But it seems like

29

... if you fall in love ... I mean, *crazy* in love ... with someone that you hardly know ... and you're just, like you can't keep your hands off her! ... and then you get to know her, and she's really a terrific person, too ... why wouldn't you keep wanting her? Why wouldn't you want her *more?*

ALAN. ... I don't know.

NICK. Yeah, see the only reason I can think of is, she's not the one. Even though in a lotta ways I think she *is* the one. But it's just gotta be that somewhere, there's one woman that I *would* feel all that for, all at the *same time* ... loving, liking, really ... loving just to talk to her, and *be* with her, be totally at ease ... and still, really, really *want* her ... I mean, with somebody like that ... I think it's possible for love, that early love that's like the best dream anybody ever had ... to *last* ... and *grow* ... you know? *(Alan's dubious, doesn't answer. Beat; the phone rings. Nick goes. Lights up on women. Lydia has the phone. Karla watches, nervous.)* Hello?

LYDIA. *(Blurts.)* Hi, who's this, is this Nick?

NICK. *(An unknown female voice. Interested:)* Yuh? *(Lydia laughs evilly, hangs up.)*

NICK. Hello? ...

KARLA. Why did you do that? You were supposed to ask for Alan!

LYDIA. *(Laughing.)* I lost my head!

NICK. *(Hangs up.)* What the hell?

LYDIA. Oh God, I shoulda said, "Is your refrigerator running?"

ALAN. What wazzat?

KARLA. Oh my God ... *(Despairs, head in hands. Lydia giggles.)*

NICK. She hung up.

ALAN. Shouldn't have identified yourself, it might be terrorists. *(Nick ignores this, wondering...)*

LYDIA. Here, lemme try again—

KARLA. *(Grabs phone.)* Give me that!

LYDIA. Come on, I just wanna—

KARLA. I will call him! ... *(Dials, as Lydia tries to stop laughing.)*

NICK. That wasn't Karla's voice.

ALAN. *(Surprised.)* Karla? That writer? You seeing her again?

NICK. *(Annoyed.)* Why wouldn't I be seeing her?

ALAN. I dunno, you usually don't keep them around that long—

NICK. *(Exploding.)* Jesus Christ, what am I, Bluebeard? *(Nick stomps out, as the phone rings.)*

KARLA. Shut up! It's ringing! *(Lydia stifles laughter.)*

ALAN. Hey, Nick! ... NICK! *(Beat; the phone rings again and the sound of a door slam is heard as Nick departs.)*

ALAN. Ooo-kaaaay ... *(Goes to phone, picks it up as:)*

KARLA. I feel sick.

ALAN. *(Ironic.)* Hello?

KARLA. *(Stopped for a beat, then:)* Alan?

ALAN. *(Looks at phone; cautious:)* Yeah?

KARLA. *(Greatly relieved.)* ... You don't know me...

ALAN. Riiiiiight...?

KARLA. But ... I need a favor. Nick has a manuscript of mine ... and I need it back.

ALAN. So ... you want me to ask him—?

KARLA. No.

ALAN. ... Oh. *(Beat; then:)* You're Karla, right? *(Fade, as sound and voices are heard:)*

Scene VI

KARLA'S VOICE. Come on in — watch out for that pail — this was so nice of you to—

ALAN'S VOICE. Hey, no problem—
KARLA'S VOICE. — there's junk everywhere, you sort of have to pick your way —
ALAN'S VOICE. You moving out?
KARLA'S VOICE. Just cleaning.
ALAN'S VOICE. Women are amazing.

(Lights up. They are entering Karla's apartment from the Offstage door. Alan carries a large manuscript in a manila envelope. Karla wears rubber gloves. Onstage is a pail of suds, a mop and a lawn-size trash bag stuffed to the brim, signs of drastic cleaning.)

KARLA. Well, I *don't* clean, ordinarily, I mean I've hardly washed my windows since I started writing. Years ago. So I got some Windex and now I'm on a roll, I'm throwing everything away and scrubbing the hell out of anything that's left. Like walls. Except I'm also thinking I might paint them. Or else chip 'em all down to the brick. I can't decide. What do you think?
ALAN. Tonight?
KARLA. Well, maybe, yeah. I may never do this again.
ALAN. Uh-huh. Well, I'd go with the paint.
KARLA. That's what I sort of ... Would you hold onto this thing while I get these down? *(She climbs on the stool to get the curtains down as Alan tucks the manuscript under his arm and balances the stool. Meanwhile she goes on:)* I've had these lousy curtains since I *got* this apartment! I made them from a sheet, you know? I must have been out of my mind.
ALAN. ... I don't know ... they're kind of...
KARLA. God, I can't wait to burn them. How could I go that long without ever *looking* at them? *(She lifts curtains off hooks, rod and all, as Alan sees something at the top of the trash bag, with one hand lifts it up: an unopened bottle of champagne. Hmm...)* Heads up! *(She drops the curtain rod and curtain as Alan drops the bottle in the bag.)* Comin' atcha. *(He helps her down. She takes the manuscript, saying:)* Oh, I'd better take that.
ALAN. Right. *(Silent, awkward transfer, then:)*

KARLA. Thanks a lot, really.

ALAN. Sure.

KARLA. I guess I was lucky to get you at home. Nick said you travel with a children's play?

ALAN. Yup.

KARLA. What play is it—?

ALAN. So you're a writer!

KARLA. Yeah.

ALAN. What's really going on in Nicaragua?

KARLA. Oh no, not that kind of writer. I don't know what's going on anywhere. I just make things up. That's all I've done since Reagan was elected.

ALAN. Well, that's one way to handle it.

KARLA. *(Chucks manuscript under the couch.)* Some life for an adult! *(Starts jerking curtains off the rod.)*

ALAN. Yeah, well, I'm twenty-nine, and I'm still playing Mr. Magic Man. And look at Nick. *(Regrets this.)* Uh ... well ... but I mean, you've seen him on TV, one piece of garbage after another ... *(She's shaking her head no.)* He's all over the frigging thing, how could you miss him?

KARLA. I don't have a television.

ALAN. You don't have...? *(Bursts out laughing.)* Oh God, that is *great!* No wonder you've got Nick chewing on the furniture! *(This news throws her, pleasantly. She turns away, jamming curtains into trash bag. Alan catches himself:)* Listen, I'm sorry, that was really crude—

KARLA. Anyway, that's over. Living in a daydream, I mean — I'm completely broke. So I got an outside job. And I mean outside. I'm a messenger, I started yesterday—

ALAN. A *messenger? I'm* a messenger! I didn't train for it or anything, but when I'm really broke—

KARLA. You are? It's terrifying, isn't it?

ALAN. Oh yeah, it's living on the edge—

KARLA. It's like a land rush out there! Only nobody knows where the land *is,* so they're rushing in all directions, all at once—

ALAN. Avoid the garment district, it's those speeding racks of bridal gowns that'll do you in.

KARLA. But you know what? I sort of like it!

ALAN. So do I!

KARLA. I feel essential to the city! Like the whole thing would collapse if I stayed home!

ALAN. Yeah, right! And I love going into offices where everybody's working — the grownups hard at it—

KARLA. Industry clacking away—

ALAN. — and I swoop right out again! Zorro! Away!

KARLA. You want a beer?

ALAN. You bet!

KARLA. *(Starts for Off R. kitchen area.)* And you can tell me, give me tips and—

ALAN. Bring your maps, I'll show you routes — *(The door buzzer sounds.)*

KARLA. That's the super — COME ON IN! — he's gonna take this trash down for me — Are you hungry?

ALAN. Always.

KARLA. Lemme just see ... what I ... *(Goes out, calling back:)* It's just no-name beer!

ALAN. My brand! *(Nick enters. He's upset but not surprised at seeing Alan. Alan's floored.)*

KARLA'S VOICE. *(Offstage.)* And I can't get to the glasses, so ... I thought I used to have some crackers ... Oh, well. Sorry...

ALAN. Hi.

NICK. *Hi. (Karla enters with two cans marked "BEER." She stops dead. Beat; she shoves the two beers at the two of them and exits to the kitchen.)* What the hell is going on?

ALAN. You tell me. *(Cracks and swigs beer.)*

NICK. Don't be cute, Al. What are you doing here?

ALAN. She asked me to come.

NICK. What for?

ALAN. She'll tell you if—

NICK. I can't believe you're pulling this—

ALAN. *Pulling* ... Nick. What do you want? Do you have any idea

34

what the fuck you want?

NICK. *(Beat; then:)* Yes. Now, I know—

ALAN. Oh, today, you know! Give me a break! *(Slams down beer can, starts out.)*

NICK. Hey, you can't just walk outa here—

ALAN. She doesn't need this! *(Exits.)*

KARLA'S VOICE. *(Offstage. Sadly.)* BYE, ALAN! THANK YOU! *(Pause. Karla enters. Silence.)*

KARLA. I thought you were the super.

NICK. Or you wouldn't've let me in? *(Pause.)* He left his book right by the phone. With your name right there. Are you ... how did you ... you're not *seeing* Al?

KARLA. Would that bother you?

NICK. Are you kidding?

KARLA. *Why? (Pause.)*

NICK. All I do is think about you, Karla. When I went home last night, I couldn't sleep and ... I ... I had fantasies about you ... *(She stares at him.)* I know...

KARLA. Why would you have fantasies about somebody you can't bring yourself to sleep with?!

NICK. I don't know, I don't know what I'm doing—

KARLA. And what about the first time, when you disappeared for two months! And then suddenly you're on the phone — "Karla, I have to see you!"

NICK. Yeah, I know—

KARLA. So I'm supposed to — and I did! And then you dump on me *again* — and here you are—

NICK. Yeah, I know, I know! I was ... confused, I *am* confused, okay? I mean I know I am! It isn't you, it's me! ... But now I'm sure of one thing ... that I ... care for you, I mean I think it's, this is *real*, and ... but I'm all fucked up! But *this* time, I really want to change it—

KARLA. *This* time? ... Oh my God. Have you done this before? To other women?

NICK. Not like this. I mean, it's happened that I've ... you know, thought I was in love, and then ... realized I wasn't, really ... but I

35

mean, that can happen to anybody...

KARLA. *(Softly, stunned.)* Oh my God ... how many times?

NICK. ... Yeah, okay ... a couple ... well ... maybe more than...

KARLA. Oh my God...

NICK. But not like this! I mean, all the other ones ... they didn't really matter — God, I sound like Kenny Rogers! But I think it's the truth! ... I *like* you, I *respect* you ... I never felt like this, like I was losing something great ... and ... *(Trails off, then, simply:)* This time I came back. *(Pause.)* I want to try to do this. But it'll take some time, because ... I'm so mixed up, you know? And maybe you don't even want to hear about it — you must be sick of this! *(Pause. Finally:)*

KARLA. I feel like you took me up to the top of a building and showed me the view, and then you pushed me off.

NICK. *(Beat; very quietly:)* Yeah, I guess you would. *(A longish pause. Then:)* Well ... I'll go ... *(Waits a moment. Nothing, so he starts for the door.)*

KARLA. *(Looks after him, expressionless:)* Bye, Nick.

NICK. *(Very subdued.)* Bye. *(He's out. A moment, then she goes to the trash bag, pulls out the bottle of champagne:)*

KARLA. I shouldn't have let him in. *(Fade, as voices are heard:)*

Scene VII

LYDIA'S VOICE. Oh my God. You are flat-ass nuts!

KARLA'S VOICE. I *said* I wasn't sure yet what I—

LYDIA'S VOICE. *(Overlap.)* This guy is the jerk of jerks, the ultimate—

KARLA'S VOICE. *(Overlap.)* He's very mixed up, but he's trying to—

LYDIA'S VOICE. Mixed up?!

(Lights up on Karla and Lydia walking in the park on a chilly Sunday afternoon, several days after Karla saw Alan and Nick.)

LYDIA. That crack he made about the sheets? "Ooh, that must feel incredible, all over!" And then he doesn't want to screw?! The guy's a psychopath! ... You know, you better find out what happened to his last true love! She probably ended up in a trunk!

KARLA. Why are you so hard on Nick? He's scared, that's all, he doesn't trust his feelings—

LYDIA. You think he's tortured, don't you? That's what they all want us to think! Well, he isn't tortured — he's just one more emotional mugger, and he's mugged you twice! Why go for three?

KARLA. Because I am obsessed with him! I can't concentrate to write, I haven't written anything since the night I met him! Writing is what I do, it's who I *am*, and I can't do it now! ... And I'm a lousy messenger, when I should be on Wall Street handing out these stupid envelopes, I'm wandering in Nick's neighborhood! Writing his name on receipts! It's so humiliating! So I try to shake it off! I run around town like a maniac! I go to everything that's free, I walk for miles, I'm swimming at the Y! I tore apart my whole apartment, I threw so much stuff away, I can't make coffee anymore! You know what I was doing yesterday, when Alan came? I was in the bathrom on my hands and knees, scrubbing around those little nuts on the base of the toilet with a toothbrush! *That* is masochism! *Anything* is better than—

LYDIA. *Find another man!*

KARLA. I tried! I went to a bar! I *did!* I talked to two nice, okay men. They both had little plastic cards which said that they did not have AIDS. I didn't have a card myself. I think they were relieved. They could just relax and try to sell each other co-ops. Or futures, or soybean shares or krugerrands or some—

LYDIA. Yeah, right.

KARLA. Anyway, it's pointless. I'm in love with Nick! I can't just swivel and refocus, like a lamp—

LYDIA. See, I don't think you are in love with Nick. You told me,

37

in some ways, you don't even like him! I think you just wanta get laid for a change! And I mean, *right on!* That's all those jerks are good for, so go for it--

KARLA. *(Overlap.)* Lydia. You are not listening. Look! I'm not saying he's the person I would choose to be in love with ... knowing what I know at this point, God! ... But I can't stop now! I've gone so far with him already. And he needs so much from me. If I just go a little farther ... give a little more ... maybe...

LYDIA. Maybe you can change him? *(Long Bronx cheer.)*

KARLA. Don't you think it's barely possible that he might really love me? *(Lydia won't deal with that one.)* I mean, I think it's possible! I think he does. Do you know how that feels? I thought I'd never get to have that! ... All right, he's scared. Well, so am I! But if we can just get past this—

LYDIA. Then you'll be together. Forever, right? Forever, with an asshole! He's a major asshole, Karla! And he doesn't like to screw! So junk him! *(Pause.)*

KARLA. You know, I'm really tired of hearing you ridicule my sex life.

LYDIA. You don't have a sex life. Even when you have a lover, you don't have a sex life. This is a problem—

KARLA. How would you describe your sex life? Tag team wrestling? ... *(Lydia gives her a bitter smile.)* They're all married, aren't they?

LYDIA. Married men are low-risk.

KARLA. Right, in every sense. All your men are married, or they're assholes, or they're both. Disqualified, right from the start—

LYDIA. *(Slings bag on to go.)* I'm off to meet Robert ... a married asshole, but he loves to screw—

KARLA. And you don't tell me about all of them, right? How many guys have you slept with in the last three months?

LYDIA. We call that a quarter in the business world.

KARLA. How many? Three? ... Five? ... More than five? ... *Ten?* ... You call that healthy?

LYDIA. You should talk! You're chasing that jerk because it's never going to happen! I've known you for a long time, Karla. You'd rather crawl on your hands and knees on broken glass than walk. *(Lydia exits, leaving Karla speechless.)*

(Crossfade to Nick's apartment. Nick and Alan are reading the Sunday paper in a frigid silence. Nick throws the paper aside, looks at Alan. Alan increases his concentration, face expressionless.)

NICK. You know, you could have told me sooner that that was all it was.
ALAN. *(Beat; then:)* What?
NICK. That manuscript. *(Pause.)*
ALAN. So now you're seeing her again?
NICK. Since when are you so interested in my affairs?
ALAN. Since I met one. *(Beat; then:)* I figured they were all...
NICK. What?
ALAN. Twits. With huge jugs.
NICK. Thanks a lot!

(Lights up on Karla on the street, standing by a pay phone, in turmoil. Suddenly she picks it up and dials. As she dials:)

ALAN. But I guess they're just masochists.
NICK. What did she say about me?
ALAN. Nothing, Nick. We didn't talk about you. *(Nick looks at him.)* Are you seeing her again? *(The phone rings, beside Alan. Alan picks it up.)* Yuh.
KARLA. Nick? *(Alan knows the voice — stonefaced, he hands the phone to Nick, sits and pretends to read the paper again.)*
NICK. Hello?
KARLA. Hi, it's me. It's Karla.
NICK. *(Wishing Alan would get the hell out.)* ...Hi...
KARLA. Look, I ... if what you said the other night is...
NICK. ...Yeah?...
KARLA. ... still goes ... let's try it.
NICK. Yeah? Ohhh ... great!

KARLA. But I mean, I'm scared, Nick, I don't wanta—

NICK. *(Overlapping.)* No, I know, I — don't worry, okay?

KARLA. But I do feel so much for you, it just seems stupid not to—

NICK. Yeah, right. Me, too. When—?

KARLA. Tonight.

NICK. *(Taken aback.)* Well ... that's ... couldn't we—?

KARLA. No. Because you have to realize, I don't want you for a friend. I can't stop there.

NICK. *(Beat, then:)* Okay ... but—

KARLA. And you said you needed time to—

NICK. Yeah, I mean I—

KARLA. Well, there isn't time. I can't be waiting like this. It's just too hard for me.

NICK. ... Well ... yeah, I ... but...

KARLA. So if you come tonight — you have to want that too. And if you don't — it's over, Nick. That's it. *(Pause.)*

NICK. Wow.

KARLA. Yeah, I know. But ... yeah. *(Pause.)*

NICK. Okay. Okay, I'll be there.

KARLA. *(Faintly.)* Bye. *(Both hang up, wiped out. Karla lets out a painful breath as Nick stands for a beat, then impulsively looks at Alan to say something. Alan gives him a cool look over the paper: no help there. Nick shuts down, exits. Lights fade.)*

INTERMISSION

ACT TWO
Scene VIII

KARLA'S APARTMENT. Early evening.

Karla enters, in her coat, carrying a grocery bag. She is totally focused on the night ahead, in a state alternating between zombie inertia and agitated action. She enters slowly, stands in the middle of the room, completely lost in daydreams. Music fades in. Karla abruptly focuses, sets down the grocery bag, takes out a smaller bag, unwraps two champagne flutes, sets them on a small table, looks at them, takes a deep breath, lets it out, takes the grocery bag and exits. Faint light maintains on glasses as lights up on:

NICK'S APARTMENT.

Nick enters, in a similar zombie-manic state. He's just taken a shower and changed his clothes. He comes in slowly, eyes blank, stops. His eyes focus, move to the phone. He goes to the phone, puts his hand on it, then stops, torn, thinking. Alan enters, gets the rest of the newspaper.

ALAN. Expecting a phone call?
NICK. *(Takes hand off phone; quick beat, then:)* I'm going out to run.
ALAN. *(As Nick goes quickly out.)* You just took a shower. *(Beat; then Alan exits with paper as:)*

KARLA'S APARTMENT.

In her bathrobe, she re-enters from kitchen, carrying a lot of hors d'oeuvres on plates, sets them around the glasses. They overflow the table. She shuffles plates, getting more nervous, puts some stuff on one plate to take back to the kitchen, then puts some of it back on the table. As this continues:

IN NICK'S APARTMENT.

Nick re-enters, goes straight to his address book by the phone, flips it open, sees a name and number, dials fast.

NICK. Susan? This is Nick. Listen, I know it's been — *(She hangs up. He's shocked, hangs up.)*

IN KARLA'S APARTMENT.

She realizes she's obsessing, takes the plate and exits.

NICK'S APARTMENT.

He looks at the address book, sees a name, just starts to reach for the phone, then hesitates ... then slings away the book.

KARLA'S APARTMENT.

She re-enters, dressed, very anxious, perches on the bed, looks at the hors d'oeuvres, gets up, picks up another plate, starts back to the kitchen, then abruptly turns back, removes all the plates and the champagne flutes and exits.

NICK'S APARTMENT.

Nick hasn't moved. Alan enters, stirring something in a saucepan. He looks at NICK. No response. He turns to go.

NICK. Al.
ALAN. Yuh. *(Pause.)*
NICK. The shower head is screwing up again.
ALAN. Oh, yeah?
NICK. Why are we paying so much fucking rent if nothing works?
ALAN. You tell me. *(Pause.)*

NICK. *(To himself.)* I need to eat, I'm ... What is that?

ALAN. Tapioca.

NICK. Christ. *(Rises.)* Let's get outa here, ya wanta? Get a burger and a couple—

ALAN. Don't you have a date?

NICK. *(Beat; then:)* ... Well, it's ... I'm not sure what I'm...

ALAN. You know what you want now—

NICK. BACK OFF, AL! *(Beat; then:)* She's putting all this pressure on me, I don't need you doing it!

ALAN. I like her, Nick. I think she's okay.

NICK. Well ... great, yeah ... but you don't know all of it. She's really pushing me, she's like ... I can't just force myself to feel something if it isn't there!

ALAN. Then why don't you leave her alone?

NICK. She doesn't want me to!

ALAN. That's why?

NICK. What do you know about women? *(Alan gestures: hey, you got me there! Long beat; Nick regrets this; softening.)* It's been a while for you, I mean, so you just think they're great. And they are — but they expect a *lot.* It's like, no matter what you do for 'em, they want more — like, what's next? They always want to know the *plan* ... and they're *all* like that! Even when they start out great, they turn into these *whiners* ... they always want to talk about who feels what, and why, and ... I mean, most of the time, I don't *know* what I feel! So when I do, right at the start, it's great, it's just fantastic, it's the only time I'm ... but then ... *(Trails off, confused, just stands there. Alan watches Nick, less judgmentally, more like, "This guy's a mess.")*

KARLA'S APARTMENT.

Karla re-enters. She's a wreck: where is he? Suddenly she goes to the phone, quickly dials Nick's number, then hangs up before it rings. She has to do something, goes quickly Offstage.

NICK'S APARTMENT.

Nick moves to the phone, uncertainly, then stops, immobilized, hand on the receiver. Alan watches.

KARLA'S APARTMENT.

Karla re-enters, grimly, with an ironing board, and sets it up.

NICK'S APARTMENT.

ALAN. *(Gently.)* Nick.
NICK. *(In a trance.)* Yeah.
ALAN. You should go, you know? *(Nick sweeps the phone onto the floor and exits. Alan stands there. Then he goes to the phone and rights it, as:)*

KARLA'S APARTMENT.

Karla marches to the phone and dials.

ACTION CONTINUES IN BOTH APARTMENTS:

Alan sets the receiver on the phone. It rings.

ALAN. Right. *(Into phone.)* Yuh.
KARLA. Nick?
ALAN. Karla.
KARLA. Yes!
ALAN. No.
KARLA. You're not coming.
ALAN. It's just me. It's Alan.
KARLA. Oh ... Alan. I'm sorry.
ALAN. Right.
KARLA. Is Nick...?
ALAN. Nope, he went out.
KARLA. Oh, good, he's coming over.
ALAN. Yeah?

KARLA. *(Beat; then:)* Oh, well ... never mind, good grief. How are you, anyway?

ALAN. I'm making tapioca.

KARLA. Huh.

ALAN. Listen. *(Long beat; then:)* Maybe ... sometime ... we could talk. You know? ... Buy ya a beer. *(Pause.)*

KARLA. Alan.

ALAN. Yuh.

KARLA. He might show up here any minute.

ALAN. Sure.

KARLA. Or I might just iron all night.

ALAN. I could bring my shirts.

KARLA. Would you like to—

ALAN. Yes.

KARLA. But we don't have to *talk*. I mean ... we can just ... talk, you know?

ALAN. *(Smiles, then.)* Oh! I just remembered — I'm bringing something. Bye. *(They both hang up as: Crossfade to:)*

Scene IX

A BAR. Later that night.

The window frame is U., with a fern hanging on it. D. are two stools and a horizontal plank: the bar.

Nick is drinking a double scotch. He's angry and depressed, and trying to get drunk, without success.

Lydia passes the window U. of the bar, glances in, exits. Beat. She re-enters, passes more slowly, looking through the window, exits again. Beat. She returns and stands blatantly staring through the window. She enters. She's quite drunk but carrying

45

it off. She considers Nick — he's possible — sees no one else, so takes the stool beside him.

LYDIA. Hi. *(Nick takes a long beat, then turns, gives her a direct, assessing look — she's possible — but he remains cool; she can do the work.)*

NICK. Hi.

LYDIA. Where's the bartender? Did he go home or what?

NICK. He's in the back, he'll be out pretty soon.

LYDIA. What do we do in the meantime? Climb over and help ourselves? *(Looks at his drink.)* What have you got?

NICK. Scotch.

LYDIA. Mmmmmm...

NICK. *(Forced.)* Be my guest.

LYDIA. How does this mix with margaritas? I got fed Mex food tonight, so I'm running on margaritas now.

NICK. I wouldn't recommend it.

LYDIA. No guts, no glory. *(Large swallow; then, charming, intimate:)* Mmmmmm ... You're an ace. We used to say that in high school. "You're an ace, dude. You're all class." Can I keep this? I'll buy you one. If they're still selling it. *(Suddenly calls Offstage to bartender:)* YOOHOO! IS THIS A DISPLAY? ARE THESE BOTTLES PAINTED ON, OR WHAT?

NICK. Sssh, sssh, hey, no, that's okay—

LYDIA. Wadaya mean, I'll buy you one, come on! Really. I paid off my Mastercard today, and I can't stand it, I gotta get back in debt. I feel naked, you know what I mean?

NICK. *(Has to smile.)* ... Yeah, I do...

LYDIA. Are you in debt? I've been in debt ever since I left Grand Rapids. Where'd you come here from?

NICK. *(Beat; then:)* It sorta doesn't matter. I'm a New Yorker now.

LYDIA. New Yorkers are born in their buildings. Where were you born?

NICK. ...Idaho.

LYDIA. Jesus.

NICK. Yeah, he's very big out there.

LYDIA. *(Likes this.)* Oh, yeah? ... No, but you know what I pic ture when I picture Idaho?

NICK. What?

LYDIA. Nothing.

NICK. ... Well, sure ... although, actually, it's beautiful—

LYDIA. I mean, I don't even have a picture for it. Or no — I see a potato. On the sixth grade map. You know? Like, state outline ... potato. *(Looks at him.)* Idaho. My God.

NICK. *(Nettled.)* Well, okay, but I mean, what about Grand Rapids?

LYDIA. What about it? *(Evil laugh.)*

NICK. ... You know ... I think I've heard your voice before.

LYDIA. I wouldn't rule it out. "You come here often?"

NICK. *(Knows this game.)* I live in the neighborhood.

LYDIA. Yeah, me too ... on and off...

NICK. But ... you probably don't realize this ... it's kind of a meat market—

LYDIA. You're joshing me—-

NICK. And I'm not into all that—

LYDIA. Oh, me either. "Gee, is this a bar? Scotch? What is scotch? Mmm, it's so *good!*" *(Nick laughs. Crossfade to:)*

KARLA'S APARTMENT. Lights include faint black-and-white TV wash from a small TV. Karla and Alan are watching an old movie, drinking champagne, eating hors d'oeuvres. As music swells:

TV VOICE. I give you the keys to the castle of my family! I will never return to this village! You will nevermore be troubled by the name Frankenstein!

ALAN. *(As music continues.)* Don't bet on it, guys.

KARLA. What village? There's no village left! You sure that isn't Basil Rathbone?

ALAN. That's a Basil Rathbone *type.* This movie is *cheap.*

KARLA. But it was swell! I *miss* television!

ALAN. Uh-oh. Down the greasy chute.

KARLA. But it's better back in Michigan. On my hometown channel, right before the sign-off, this lady, Mrs. Yursik, she goes to our church, she comes on and gives a recipe.

ALAN. Before the *sign-off?*

KARLA. Yeah. For Tuna Puff or one of those. Then a whole bunch of Marines come on and sing "The Star-Spangled Banner."

ALAN. *(Beat; then:)* You do the recipe, I'll sing—

KARLA. But I can sing the high part!

ALAN. What? Get outa here, six people in America can sing the high part — *(Karla starts singing the high part, over the TV sound. Alan sings mock bass. Then Karla breaks off, laughing, turns TV off.)*

KARLA. Oh, God, we better shut up, it must be late! *(Silence. They're still smiling but a little shy: what's next?)*

ALAN. Yeah... and I'm off to Sunflower Town at dawn. *(Sees her expression.)* The kid show.

KARLA. *(Forboding.)* "Sunflower Town?"

ALAN. You got it.

KARLA. Wow... But is it fun at least, are the actors nice?

ALAN. Nice? ... Yeah ... I guess ... at heart. But it does things to you. Like the woman who plays the princess. She's supposed to be sixteen, you know? A *princess*. But she's gotta be forty, at least. She's been playing it for eighteen years or something. Carries a flask of cointreau at all times. Drinks it in the car.

KARLA. Poor thing.

ALAN. Then there's this guy Rory, he's like the kid show Hitler, won't let the women piss. And last time we went out, all three women wound up sleeping with him ... Women are such masochists, I — ... *(Regrets this. Quickly:)* Not that I can talk. I once toured Alabama with a one-man puppet show. Had this old car, with all the puppets in the trunk. And I'd set up my stage in parking lots, and pass a hat.

KARLA. That sounds pretty chancy.

ALAN. It's not even sanitary ... and I didn't blame 'em. It was a rotten puppet show. The puppets were old and falling apart, some

48

of 'em were almost bald, they looked diseased, you know? This one day, I was doing the after-Slurpee show in the 7-11 lot, and I happened to glance down at the cast — I usually didn't do that, I tried to avoid their eyes — and one of the puppets had lost his head. It was sorta ... dangling off to the side, like this ... *(Demonstrates.)* But since I was the soul of the puppet, so to speak, he was still talking away in his strange little voice, my "talking through peanut butter" voice, and still jiggling away in his lifelike little dance.

KARLA. What did the audience say?

ALAN. Nothing. They didn't seem to care. That was my epiphany about the theatre. So I went on with the show!

KARLA. You have courage, Alan.

ALAN. *(Smiles.)* It comes and goes.

KARLA. ... I know ... *(Pause. a possibility is there. Both contemplate it, but each waits for the other to do something, if anything. Crossfade to:)*

THE BAR. Nick is returning to the stool from Offstage. Both he and Lydia have fresh drinks.

NICK. The kitchen's closed. I need to eat. You interested in eating?

LYDIA. *(Bitterly.)* I got fed Mex food.

NICK. ... Right ... but would you want to—?

LYDIA. *(Brooding.)* Some men have no class.

NICK. ... Yeah ... well...

LYDIA. And I couldn't go straight home and stare at the walls after that, right?

NICK. *(True.)* Doesn't sound that great to me—

LYDIA. Because I did that last night, you know? Stared at the walls, drank a bottle of wine, colored in my coloring book. I have this collection of esoteric coloring books. Like, "The Heroines of the Bronte Novels Coloring Book." They're great for when you can't sleep.

NICK. ... I don't think I've ever seen—

LYDIA. So I did that for a while. Then I watched part of this old movie. Nurse movie. World War II. I couldn't follow it. But it was all women, there were no men in the movie at all. And in the end, they all laid down their lives. I sorta figured that was coming when I saw there weren't any men in the movie, you know what I mean?

NICK. No.

LYDIA. Those all-women movies. They blow them all to smithereens, or the plane goes down. They go nobly and heroically. But they get rid of the cunts.

NICK. ... You know ... guys get killed in movies too. It's *mostly* guys. Not to mention *wars*, I mean—

LYDIA. Then I scrubbed the kitchen *floor* ... that's how bored I was! Not bored. Just ... *(Great frustration.)*

NICK. Right. Well, everybody gets—

LYDIA. And the reason I couldn't sleep in the first place, it wasn't my fault for once! That's the worst part when you can't sleep, you feel like it's all your fault. Like, "If I wasn't so fucking neurotic, I'd be asleep by now," you know?

NICK. I gotta admit, I don't have trouble sleeping, myself. *(Lydia gives him a dark look.)* I guess you want to tell me whose fault it was?

LYDIA. Oh, why bother, you know?

NICK. Right, yeah, so can we get outa here—?

LYDIA. *(Overlapping.)* It was the same old thing. This guy I saw a coupla times, he calls me up last night at two o'clock in the morning! Woke me up! I mean, I was asleep for once, and this asshole calls me up, wants to come right over! I mean ... this guy! ... he doesn't call me, like, for a month, you know? And then all of the sudden at two o'clock in the morning, here he is on the phone, "I have to see you!" *(Silenced, Nick stares at her.)* So I said no! Right? "No, you asshole! No! Fuck off!" ... So then I couldn't sleep. Of course, of course.

NICK. *(Has had enough; anger building:)* ... You know ... maybe you should try putting yourself in this guy's shoes, for once. I mean, *why* does he back off, you know? Like maybe you come on too strong, ever think of that? ... I mean, women are *scary* now! Maybe you need to give this guy a little breathing room! Or maybe he's insecure, he doesn't call because he thinks you'll give him hell — which is, you know, what happened, so—

LYDIA. *I'm* insecure! It's crap like that that *makes* me insecure!

NICK. Well, sure, but it's a two-way street—

LYDIA. *(Overlap.)* And then tonight this other jerk — Oh, screw. You'll just stick up for him, too.

NICK. I'm not sticking up for him, I'm just saying it works both ways—

LYDIA. It works both ways for *you. (Tense pause. Both drink. Crossfade to:)*

KARLA'S APARTMENT. As before.

ALAN. Karla ... *(She looks at him. Not what he wants to say:)* ... Want me to leave this TV here? We've got a bigger one, needless to say. Huge. Color. Cable. Movie channels. VCR—

KARLA. Oh... thanks, but I don't want it here. I'm afraid it'll suck out my brains while I'm sleeping.

ALAN. Right.

KARLA. But you shouldn't go home this late with a television ... *(Pause. The possibility is right there. But neither makes a move. Crossfade to:)*

THE BAR. Nick starts to put his jacket on. Lydia registers this and switches gears.

LYDIA. *(Charming, wry.)* Hey. Sorry. Really.

NICK. *(Continues putting jacket on.)* Hey, no problem—

LYDIA. No, that was dumb, you know? The truth is, I came in here kind of bummed out... *really* bummed out, really down ... but you were cool, you listened ... and I mean, you're right, when I get hurt and mad like that, I just don't wanta see the other side, you know? But I know there's another side. I know that, you know?

NICK. Sure.

LYDIA. And you were great. God, you gave me your drink, you

know? I drank the whole thing. I'm a little greedy that way. I can be ...excesive, you know? When I'm in this mood.

NICK. Sure. Right.

LYDIA. Thanks. You're not married, are you?

NICK. *(Strange question.)* No.

LYDIA. I still feel safe with you. *(Holds his look.)* You don't feel very safe with me.

NICK. *(Smiles.)* No.

LYDIA. But sometimes that's okay, you know? *(This is true. Pause.)*

LYDIA. And I'm pretty picky. That may surprise you. But I am. Selective, you know?

NICK. Yeah?

LYDIA. You're a nice man.

NICK. I'd like to think so.

LYDIA. *(Rests a hand on his thigh.)* Good ... then we'll both think so. *(Pause.)*

NICK. *(Wavering.)* Uh ... look, I'm an actor, and I've got a shoot tomorrow, so—

LYDIA. Uh-huh. Well, I'd say "Tell me all about yourself," but I'm sorta sleepy, you know? *(Nick understands only too well. They're his terms, but he also wants to sock her. Lights up on Karla's apartment, lights maintain on bar.)*

IN THE APARTMENT:

KARLA. Alan.

ALAN. Yeah?

KARLA. I don't know what to do.

IN THE BAR:

LYDIA. It's getting pretty late, you know. Almost closing time.

IN THE APARTMENT:

ALAN. I'm not exactly the one to ask, you know ... *(Karla gives a small laugh.)*

IN THE BAR.

NICK. *(Hostile beneath the charm, decides.)* This dress is great ... what is it, silk?
LYDIA. Fake silk. For the working girl.
NICK. Incredible, the way it shines and clings. It must feel wonderful against your skin, all over. *(An awful bell resounds among the clouds of alcohol and lust in Lydia's brain. But she shakes it off.)*
LYDIA. ...Let's just go ... *(They get up, slowly, remaining close.)*

IN THE APARTMENT.

KARLA. *(Honest, torn.)* I really like you, Alan.
ALAN. Good.

IN THE BAR.

NICK. My name's Nick.
LYDIA. ... Oh, fuck.

IN THE APARTMENT.

Karla and Alan stand very close. She plays with the sleeve of his shirt, stuck in indecision. Alan waits.

IN THE BAR.

NICK. Are you okay?
LYDIA. No. No, I'm really not. Life sucks. And people suck, you know? *You* know.
NICK. Look, I don't need this—
LYDIA. Like I *do?!* I'm not going home alone! I don't have any booze.

NICK. Is that the problem?
LYDIA. Not for you! Evidently not!
NICK. I'm going—
LYDIA. *(In turmoil.)* No. Wait. No. Wait. Wait ...

IN THE APARTMENT.

Alan ends the moment by getting his jacket and wrapping the cord around the TV, picks it up.

IN THE BAR.

LYDIA. You don't want to know me, right?
NICK. Well, I wouldn't—
LYDIA. No, I would, I would—
NICK. That's it.
LYDIA. Right, right ... shit!

IN THE APARTMENT.

KARLA. I hate this!
ALAN. You'll get it figured out.
KARLA. I have. I mean, I know. But I've been stuck for so long that I don't know what the next move *is. (He kisses her, sweetly and gently, with the TV still under his arm.)*

IN THE BAR.

Nick makes a move away. Lydia pulls him into a passionate kiss. This holds, both couples kissing. Then:

LYDIA. *(Unsteadily, as they break:)* ... Come on ... and let's not talk, okay? *(They start out together. Lights fade on bar.)*

IN THE APARTMENT:

The kiss is getting great. Karla breaks it, but stays close.

KARLA. If you just weren't his roommate—
ALAN. I'm moving out first chance I get—
KARLA. Put the TV down. *(Music in. Slow crossfade to:)*

Scene X

LYDIA'S OFFICE. Night.

The next evening, around eight o'clock. Shadowy light fades up slowly on Lydia, sitting in the dark and looking out the window at the city far below. A moment; then Karla's voice.

KARLA'S VOICE. Lydia?
LYDIA. Here.
KARLA. *(Entering.)* Why are you sitting here in the dark?
LYDIA. I'm looking at the city. *(Karla comes to stand behind Lydia's chair. Both gaze out. Then:)*
KARLA. New York is so festive at night! There must be a billion squares of light. And the avenues are chains of light. And it's all in motion ... a great big spinning necklace!
LYDIA. This city is the only dream I ever had. When I was a kid, I never knew what I wanted to be, I just wanted to live in New York. *(Beat; then:)* Sometimes I feel like my life went to hell when I got on the bus in Grand Rapids. But ... who would I be if I weren't here?
KARLA. Yeah ... I don't know ... *(Pause. Gaze still on the city:)* when I called you this morning, I was so happy! And when I saw the sunshine, I went rushing outside, like I'd been released. Morning in the city! It smelled like bread and soap. And coffee, in those blue-and-white Greek diner cardboard cups. Everybody had a cup of coffee in one hand. That coffee smelled so good — like purpose,

like a handle on your life! *(Pause.)* You know how some days, the city is so dark, so overwhelming ... ragged people on every block, and people filled with rage ... and they're right to be so angry, they know they've been written off, it fills you with rage, too ... After a day like that, you don't want to go out again, you're hiding, in despair ... But other days, the city seems possible again, like it was when we first came here ... overwhelming in a *good* way, filled with everything in human life ... and everyone is funny and ornery and courageous ... Some days, everything seems possible again. For everyone. *(Brief pause, then:)* So I walked to the Village, and I stayed all day. Sat at that table in the playground, where I used to take my notebook when I started writing. Went and looked at our old building on East 4th. They still have those same two garbage cans. *(Lydia smiles faintly.)* And we used to say, "Some day we'll buy this brownstone. And I'll run a printing press in the basement, like Anais Nin."

LYDIA. "And I'll be upstairs, cooking succulent meals ... and interviewing the nice young men who have burning desires to write." *(Brief pause.)*

KARLA. Then I started up Sixth Avenue, and I just kept walking. The Avenue of the Americas — there's so much romance in that name! I got to 57th as it was growing dark, and I stood there on the corner ... people were rushing past me, their faces like birds streaming by ... and the streets were full of golden taxis pouring toward the park ... and I got the New York feeling! ... that it's all going on *right here!* ... and yet, *where is it?* ... It's like there's a wonderful, magical party somewhere in the city. And all these people know about it, and they're going there. And I could go too, if I knew where it was. But I'm never going to know. *(Pause.)*

LYDIA. *(Still gazing out.)* I don't know what I'd do without you, Karla. I'm a mess, a classic case. But Christ, I really love you.

KARLA. I know. I love you too. You're what keeps me here. *(Rests a hand on Lydia's shoulder.)*

LYDIA. *(Long beat; then:)* It was nice ... with Alan?

KARLA. It was so nice ... and I *trust* him! *(Long beat; then, hard to say:)* But I'm still ... I can't ... let go of Nick. *(This is a blow to Lydia.*

56

Karla goes on, painfully:) If I just knew *why* ... why he doesn't ... couldn't... He isn't a bad person, Lydia. He's probably been badly hurt, and that's why he's afraid. If I just hadn't pressed him, maybe he would have learned to trust—

LYDIA. *(Can't stand this idiocy anymore.)* I slept with him last night.

KARLA. ... Who?

LYDIA. Nick. I slept with him. I picked him up in a bar.

KARLA. ... He was with *you?* .... *Why?* Were you that angry—?

LYDIA. No, it wasn't—

KARLA. Trying to, what, show me—

LYDIA. You weren't even in it—

KARLA. Because you don't care, you'll sleep with anybody! So why would you take Nick, unless ... You didn't talk about me! I'll kill you if—

LYDIA. No! He didn't know who I was! And I practically had my hand in his pants when I found out who he—

KARLA. But you didn't let that stop you.

LYDIA. No. *(Beat; then:)* I thought about you. *(Karla laughs, painfully.)* I was drunk, and fucked up—

KARLA. I can't hear this — *(Starts to go.)*

LYDIA. And fucking Robert had just dumped me at the fucking *bus stop* so he could go meet his wife! I couldn't go home after—

KARLA. NO!! You didn't have to whore around! You could have called me! We could have talked—

LYDIA. I didn't want to talk! That wasn't what I needed!

KARLA. What about what *I* need? Did you—?

LYDIA. Yes! Yes! But I didn't take anything away from you!

KARLA. He was coming to my place last night!

LYDIA. It was practically two o'clock in the morning—

KARLA. *(Fighting knowledge.)* He might still have—

LYDIA. You are never gonna get what you want from him!

KARLA. *Why not?*

LYDIA. Because he doesn't have it! *(Beat; then:)* He's a

lightweight, Karla. *(Beat; then:)* He's not even a good lay. *(Karla gives her a terrible look.)* And he gets his kicks from holding out.

KARLA. I don't believe that he's that cruel.

LYDIA. Look at his record. *(Long beat; then:)* How long would he have made you wait—?

KARLA. Oh shut up, shut up! *(A miserable silence. Then:)*

LYDIA. *(Humbly.)* Will you come here and let me hug you?

KARLA. *(Very cold.)* I don't want you to hug me.

LYDIA. I have a hangover like death, but I've been sitting here all day, cold sober, so you could call me names.

KARLA. You think it would be over then? *(Lydia looks at her. Quietly:)* You've been the only person in the world who was always on my side. And I've been that for you. And now you've ended it.

LYDIA. Karla...

KARLA. You knew how I wanted him! How could you take him *like that!*

LYDIA. Because that's who he is. We recognized each other.

KARLA. *(Long beat; then:)* I didn't expect it from you. *(Lights fade. Sound of muffled pounding creeps in; lights up on:)*

Scene XI

NICK'S APARTMENT. An hour later, same night.

Nick's asleep on the couch in his underwear, his clothing from the previous night scattered around. Sound of muffled pounding starts Off L., grows. Nick rouses as Alan's voice is heard:

ALAN'S VOICE. *(Offstage.)* ... NICK! ... Oh Christ, don't do this to me, please, God ... NICK!!

NICK. *(Groggy.)* ... Alan? *(Slowly sits up, then stands and staggers Off L., as Alan goes on:)*

ALAN'S VOICE. *(Offstage.)* NICK!! IF YOU'RE IN THERE, LET ME IN AND I'LL FORGIVE YOU EVERYTHING! NIIIIIIIIICK!!!

NICK'S VOICE. *(Offstage. Overlapping.)* Shut up! Are you crazy! Do you want the neighbors coming out and—

ALAN'S VOICE. *(Offstage. Overlapping.)* Oh, you're here! — Oh, thank you, God! — I forgot my keys! That old lady on the first floor let me in downstairs, but I thought I might have to sleep in the hallway ... *(Alan enters, Nick behind him. Alan wears clown costume and makeup and a raincoat, carries his duffel bag.)*

NICK. You're spose to be in ... Indiana ... or...

ALAN. The goddamn car broke down again. I had to hitchhike back. *(Drops duffel, collapses on couch.)* If you've got someone here, I'm sorry, tell her I'll put my earplugs in.

NICK. You hitchhiked ... in your clown costume...?

ALAN. Where was I gonna change, in the middle of a freeway? ... Thank God some trucker picked me up. Except he made me talk like Mr. Magic Man all the way to Newark. *(Bellyflops on couch, groaning.)* Oh, home ... I'm home ... If only there were food...

NICK. Sorry.

ALAN. Please ... do me one last favor. Call "24-Hour Pizza" and ask them to send up a Mega-Pie with Double Everything. I'd do it myself, but if they were mean to me on the phone, I know I'd start to cry...

NICK. Okay ... lemme get the phone book...

ALAN. 296-1041. *(Nick gets phone, dials:)* They said they'd give us food money, but they "forgot" — HA! So we all split up to hitch, and then I realized I had sixty-seven cents. So I got this trucker to buy me some Life Savers. That's all I've had to eat all day. Life Savers. Choc-o-Mint! I was hoping he'd buy me a meal at some point, but he didn't offer. He must've been scared to walk into a truck stop with Mr. Magic Man.

NICK. *(Into phone.)* Hi, I'd like to order a Mega-Pie—

ALAN. With Double Everything—

NICK. With Double Everything. Delivered to — It *is* for Al, right. Thanks. *(Hangs up.)*

ALAN. FRIEND! *(Sticks out hand, Nick clasps it.)* When it comes, just drop it on me and I'll die content. *(The lobby buzzer sounds. They look at each other: naaah ... Nick goes to the intercom as:)*

ALAN. Must be for those coke dealers in the penthouse ... *(Groans.)*

NICK. Who is it? *(Karla's voice on intercom.)* It's Karla. I have to see you, Nick. *(Shocked silence from both. Then Alan laughs in outraged disbelief.)*

NICK. Oh, fuck! ... *(To Alan.)* Would you shut up, please? ... *(To intercom.)* Come on up. *(Alan sits up as Nick starts picking up his clothes, pulling them on:)* What time is it? What is she, crazy? ... look at this shirt ... ah, who cares ... *(Puts it on.)*

ALAN. HOW DO YOU DO IT?! HOW THE FUCK DO YOU DO IT?! I'VE ONLY BEEN GONE TWELVE HOURS!

NICK. Do what? This is not my fault — I don't wanta see her—

ALAN. It's a sickness, that's what it is — she's not responsible, she's sick — you're sick, you're very, *very* sick — and I must be sick too, or I wouldn't've gotten into this!

NICK. You're babbling, Al, you're losing it — go to bed, okay? And when the pizza comes, I'll bring it in. You want a beer or something? *(Sound of Karla's knock on door.)* Shit! — *(Calls.)* JUST A SECOND! — Where the hell'd I put my pants?

ALAN. YOUR PANTS?! WHY BOTHER?! *(Laughs maniacally.)*

NICK. Al, for God's sake, get outa here — *(Sees his pants under Alan.)* Here, get up, you're sitting on my — *(Nick bends over Alan to yank his trousers out from under him. Alan goes with a wild impulse, punches Nick in the stomach. Nick grunts, falls backward, wind knocked out, stares at Alan, astounded. Alan stares back, stunned.)*

ALAN. God, that felt fantastic! *(Karla enters, sees a large clown leaning over Nick, who's breathless, on the floor, clutching his trousers.)*

KARLA. ... Hello? ... *(Alan leaps up; she sees his makeup and crazed look, gasps.)*

60

ALAN. I can't believe it! I disabled him! You respect this man?!
(Nick tries to speak and can't.)
KARLA. ... Alan?...
ALAN. Hell, yes! I shoulda had this on last night! *(Stomps Off R.)*
KARLA. I wouldn't've come if I'd known you were still around—
ALAN'S VOICE. Hey, why hide anything from me, I'm just the sideshow! *(Sound of bedroom door slam.)*
KARLA. Did he ... he didn't hit you, did he? *(Nick can't speak, nods.)* Oh! ... that's so sweet ... *(Nick looks at her.)* But ... *(Calls.)* ALAN! YOU DON'T UNDERSTAND! *(Sound of Alan's door opening.)*
ALAN'S VOICE. *(Offstage.)* YOU'RE RIGHT ON THAT ONE! *(Sound: Slam! Nick's slowly getting to his feet. She sees this, makes a move to help him up, pulls back: doesn't want to touch him.)*
KARLA. I know it's late, but I just had to get this over with.
NICK. ... This isn't ... a great time ... to talk...
KARLA. I think I've let you talk too much. And I don't blame you for last night. That's what really makes me sick — deep down, I'm not surprised.
NICK. Any guy would panic if you pulled that "Now or never" stuff—
KARLA. But you would have come back again, with excuses, right? That's what I'll never understand. You don't want me, Nick. But you want me to want *you* — *why?*
NICK. No ... that's not...
KARLA. Then why do you keep coming back? ... you give me just enough to keep me hanging in there—
NICK. You got a whole lot out of me! But it's never enough!
KARLA. Because you gave me *everything* at first — and then you took some back! And you kept telling me that *maybe* I'd get everything again! And I had to believe it! When I met you, I'd been alone so long, I'd actually forgotten what it felt like to love some-one! But when you seemed to love me ... you called up all this pas-

sion in me — God, it just came rushing out! — and then you left me with it! And I couldn't make it stop! I was afraid to stop it, I might never have the chance to feel that way again! You couldn't know all that. But, Nick ... you didn't want me to stop. You wanted me to love you ... and to wait. How long?

NICK. God, you make me sound like a monster! ... Okay, maybe I ... I shoulda left you alone, after the first time ... but I *missed* you! And I wasn't lying, I really started to believe that you might be my chance to change—

KARLA. That won't happen. Say it, Nick. *Say it.*

NICK. ... I guess not. No.

KARLA. Thank you. Goodbye. *(Turns away toward Off R.)*

NICK. I really do have feelings for you ... *(She turns, stares at him coolly:)* ... but I don't know what they are. I'm all fucked up—

KARLA. I'm fucked up too! But I'm gonna fight it! *(Karla exits Off R., surprising Nick, as door buzzes. Nick hits the button:)*

NICK. Yeah.

KARLA'S VOICE. *(Offstage. Over sound of knock on Alan's door:)* Alan? Please, can I talk to you?

DELIVERY MAN. *(Voice on intercom.)* Gotta pizza here. *(Crossfade to:)*

Scene XII

KARLA'S APARTMENT, shortly thereafter. She enters. Lydia is there.

KARLA. *(Stops cold, then:)* How did you get in here?

LYDIA. *(Holds up keys.)* I have your keys. I've had 'em since the day we moved you in. *(Pause. Thus summed up, their history lies between them. Lights up on:)*

NICK'S APARTMENT. Very down, Nick sits alone. Alan enters, eating pizza.

ALAN. Want some pizza?
NICK. No. You ever sock me again, I'll break your fucking head.
ALAN. Right.

KARLA'S APARTMENT.

KARLA. *(Suddenly exhausted.)* I don't want to talk to you.
LYDIA. Can I have a beer for the road? *(Karla hesitates.)* Put it in
a bag. *(Karla exits to the kitchen.)*

NICK'S APARTMENT.

ALAN. I'm moving out as soon as I can find a place.
NICK. You think I'm a total shit too.
ALAN. I just think it's time.

KARLA'S APARTMENT.

*Karla re-enters, hands Lydia a beer. Lydia opens beer, takes a long
swig.*

NICK'S APARTMENT.

NICK. I didn't mean to hurt her, Al. *(No response from Alan.)* Or
else ... if I *did* mean to ... I swear I didn't know it. The way it feels is
like ... I just ... stumble into these things ... but then, somehow,
every time ... somebody gets hurt...
ALAN. Like a hit-and-run. *(Nick looks at him.)* You gotta quit
doing this. Get some help.
NICK. ... I know.

KARLA'S APARTMENT.

KARLA. Why did you have to tell me? We could've stayed
the same.
LYDIA. *(Beat; then, honest and painful:)* I would've told you some-

time ... called some night when I was drunk, to get it off my chest ... and I want you to see that jerk for what he is! ... If you have to see me, too ... well, tough.

KARLA. I don't believe that you told me for *my* sake.

LYDIA. ... A little bit, for you. *(Beat; then:)* You wouldn't take him now. *(Karla can't argue with that. Lydia holds out the beer. Karla shakes head no.)* Just a sip ... to share?

KARLA. *(Looks at her; not taking beer.)* I never will forgive you. Not deep down.

LYDIA. No, I know.

NICK'S APARTMENT.

NICK. So now *you're* seeing her?

KARLA'S APARTMENT.

LYDIA. But you finally kissed him off, right?

NICK'S APARTMENT.

ALAN. I'm gonna give her a little time first.
NICK. Yeah, well ... that's a good idea...

KARLA'S APARTMENT.

KARLA. We're not gonna talk about him. Ever again.
LYDIA. ... Fine with me.

NICK'S APARTMENT.

ALAN. I'll wait till tonight.

KARLA'S APARTMENT.

KARLA. And if you ever go near Alan — I will kill you.
LYDIA. ... Right.

FADE TO BLACK/END OF PLAY

PROP LIST

ACT I
SCENE 3
Macy's shopping bag containing:
        Colored tissue paper
        Exotically colored underpants
        Dress
        Nightie, moderately sexy
        (Perfume, bath oil and sheets not seen)
Absinth in bottle
Vermouth in bottle
Ice in ice bucket
2 tumblers
Lemon and knife or lemon slices (opt.)

SCENE 4
Simple curtains, neatly handmade from a sheet, on rod
Slim leatherbound book
Simple flowers in a peanut butter jar
Champagne in a bottle ($25-30 range)
2 plain glasses

SCENE 5
Kleenex in bathrobe pockets
2 phones, 1 in Karla's apartment, 1 in Nick's apartment
Duffel bag
Cereal bowl with food and spoon in it

SCENE 6
Large manuscript in Manila envelope
Rubber cleaning gloves
Pail of suds
Mop
Lawn-size trash bag, stuffed full
Unopened bottle of same champagne as in Scene 4
Stool
Curtains on rod (same as Scene 4)
2 cans marked "BEER" (Alan opens 1 during scene)

SCENE 7
Sections of Sunday *New York Times*
Pay phone, not realistic
Phone in Nick's apartment

ACT II
SCENE 8
Grocery bag containing:
       2 champagne flutes wrapped in paper in smaller bag
       (different wrapped hors d'oeuvres, not seen)
Same sections of Sunday *Times*
2 phones, 1 in each apartment
Hors d'oeuvres on 3 or 4 small plates
Nick's address book
Tapioca in saucepan with spoon
Ironing board

SCENE 9
Fern hanging in window
2 stools and plank for bar
Small TV
Tumbler of double scotch and ice
Champagne, hors d'oeuvres (same as Scene 7)
2nd tumbler of double scotch and ice

SCENE 11
Duffel bag
Phone in Nick's apartment
1 unopened can marked "BEER" (Lydia opens during scene)
1 large piece of overloaded pizza

SUSPENDED WINDOW
(moves around)

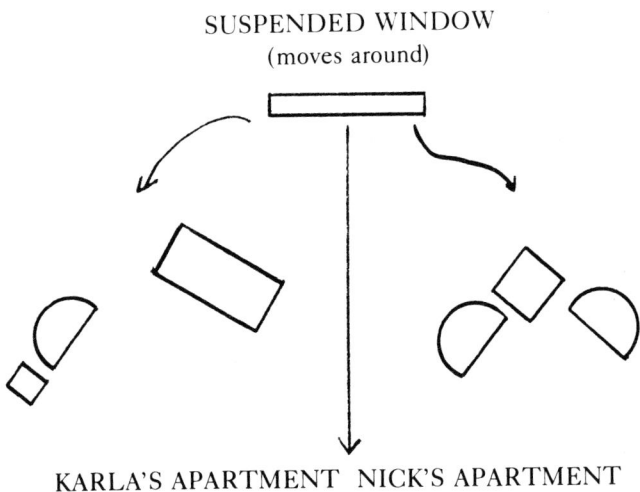

KARLA'S APARTMENT NICK'S APARTMENT

SCENE DESIGN
"LOVE MINUS"

Scenes in Lydia's office are played D.C. with 1 or 2 office chairs rolled onstage for those scenes. For Scene 3, a liquor cabinet can also be rolled on and off. The scenes outdoors are played Downstage with 1 set piece for each: a fragment of a railing for Scene 1; a fragment of a pay phone for Scene 7. The bar scene is played D.L. with 2 stools and a railing.

NEW PLAYS

- **MERE MORTALS by David Ives, author of *All in the Timing*.** Another critically acclaimed evening of one-act comedies combining wit, satire, hilarity and intellect – a winning combination. The entire evening of plays can be performed by 3 men and 3 women. ISBN: 0-8222-1632-9

- **BALLAD OF YACHIYO by Philip Kan Gotanda.** A provocative play about innocence, passion and betrayal, set against the backdrop of a Hawaiian sugar plantation in the early 1900s. *"Gotanda's writing is superb ... a great deal of fine craftsmanship on display here, and much to enjoy."* --*Variety.* *"...one of the country's most consistently intriguing playwrights..."* --*San Francisco Examiner.* *"As he has in past plays, Gotanda defies expectations..."* --*Oakland Tribune.* [3M, 4W] ISBN: 0-8222-1547-0

- **MINUTES FROM THE BLUE ROUTE by Tom Donaghy.** While packing up a house, a family converges for a weekend of flaring tempers and shattered illusions. *"With MINUTES FROM THE BLUE ROUTE [Donaghy] succeeds not only in telling a story -- a typically American one with wide appeal, about how parents and kids struggle to understand each other and mostly fail -- but in notating it inventively, through wittily elliptical, crisscrossed speeches, and in making it carry a fairly vast amount of serious weight with surprising ease."* --*Village Voice.* [2M, 2W] ISBN: 0-8222-1608-6

- **SCAPIN by Molière, adapted by Bill Irwin and Mark O'Donnell.** This adaptation of Molière's 325-year-old farce, *Les Fourberies de Scapin*, keeps the play in period while adding a late Twentieth Century spin to the language and action. *"This SCAPIN, [with a] felicitous adaptation by Mark O'Donnell, would probably have gone over big with the same audience who first saw Molière's Fourberies de Scapin...in Paris in 1671."* --*N.Y. Times.* *"Commedia dell'arte and vaudeville have at least two things in common: baggy pants and Bill Irwin. All make for a natural fit in the celebrated clown's entirely unconventional adaptation."* --*Variety* [9M, 3W, flexible] ISBN: 0-8222-1603-5

- **THE TURN OF THE SCREW adapted for the stage by Jeffrey Hatcher from the story by Henry James.** The American master's classic tale of possession is given its most interesting "turn" yet: one woman plays the mansion's terrified governess while a single male actor plays everyone else. *"In his thoughtful adaptation of Henry James' spooky tale, Jeffrey Hatcher does away with the supernatural flummery, exchanging the story's balanced ambiguities about the nature of reality for a portrait of psychological vampirism..."* --*Boston Globe.* [1M, 1W] ISBN: 0-8222-1554-3

- **NEVILLE'S ISLAND by Tim Firth.** A middle management orientation exercise turns into an hilarious disaster when the team gets "shipwrecked" on an uninhabited island. *"NEVILLE'S ISLAND ... is that rare event: a genuinely good new play..., it's a comedic, adult LORD OF THE FLIES..."* --*The Guardian.* *"... A non-stop, whitewater deluge of comedy both sophisticated and slapstick.... Firth takes a perfect premise and shoots it to the extreme, flipping his fish out of water, watching them flop around a bit, and then masterminding the inevitable feeding frenzy."* --*New Mexican.* [4M] ISBN: 0-8222-1581-0

DRAMATISTS PLAY SERVICE, INC.
440 Park Avenue South, New York, NY 10016 212-683-8960 Fax 212-213-1539
postmaster@dramatists.com www.dramatists.com

NEW PLAYS

- **TAKING SIDES by Ronald Harwood.** Based on the true story of one of the world's greatest conductors whose wartime decision to remain in Germany brought him under the scrutiny of a U.S. Army determined to prove him a Nazi. *"A brave, wise and deeply moving play delineating the confrontation between culture, and power, between art and politics, between irresponsible freedom and responsible compromise." --London Sunday Times.* [4M, 3W] ISBN: 0-8222-1566-7

- **MISSING/KISSING by John Patrick Shanley.** Two biting short comedies, MISSING MARISA and KISSING CHRISTINE, by one of America's foremost dramatists and the Academy Award winning author of *Moonstruck*. *" ... Shanley has an unusual talent for situations ... and a sure gift for a kind of inner dialogue in which people talk their hearts as well as their minds...." --N.Y. Post.* MISSING MARISA [2M], KISSING CHRISTINE [1M, 2W] ISBN: 0-8222-1590-X

- **THE SISTERS ROSENSWEIG by Wendy Wasserstein, Pulitzer Prize-winning author of *The Heidi Chronicles*.** Winner of the 1993 Outer Critics Circle Award for Best Broadway Play. A captivating portrait of three disparate sisters reuniting after a lengthy separation on the eldest's 50th birthday. *"The laughter is all but continuous." --New Yorker. "Funny. Observant. A play with wit as well as acumen.... In dealing with social and cultural paradoxes, Ms. Wasserstein is, as always, the most astute of commentators." --N.Y. Times.* [4M, 4W] ISBN: 0-8222-1348-6

- **MASTER CLASS by Terrence McNally. Winner of the 1996 Tony Award for Best Play.** Only a year after winning the Tony Award for *Love! Valour! Compassion!*, Terrence McNally scores again with the most celebrated play of the year, an unforgettable portrait of Maria Callas, our century's greatest opera diva. *"One of the white-hot moments of contemporary theatre. A total triumph." --N.Y. Post. "Blazingly theatrical." -- USA Today.* [3M, 3W] ISBN: 0-8222-1521-7

- **DEALER'S CHOICE by Patrick Marber.** A weekly poker game pits a son addicted to gambling against his own father, who also has a problem but won't admit it. *"... make tracks to DEALER'S CHOICE, Patrick Marber's wonderfully masculine, razor-sharp dissection of poker-as-life.... It's a play that comes out swinging and never lets up -- a witty, wisecracking drama that relentlessly probes the tortured souls of its six very distinctive ... characters. CHOICE is a cutthroat pleasure that you won't want to miss." --Time Out (New York).* [6M] ISBN: 0-8222-1616-7

- **RIFF RAFF by Laurence Fishburne.** RIFF RAFF marks the playwriting debut of one of Hollywood's most exciting and versatile actors. *"Mr. Fishburne is surprisingly and effectively understated, with scalding bubbles of anxiety breaking through the surface of a numbed calm." --N.Y. Times. "Fishburne has a talent and a quality...[he] possesses one of the vital requirements of a playwright -- a good ear for the things people say and the way they say them." --N.Y. Post.* [3M] ISBN: 0-8222-1545-4

DRAMATISTS PLAY SERVICE, INC.
440 Park Avenue South, New York, NY 10016 212-683-8960 Fax 212-213-1539
postmaster@dramatists.com www.dramatists.com